T0277188

Praise for *At the End of the World There Is a Pond*

"Steven Duong's sparkling debut collection entices with its vision of a pond—at once a goal, yet a finale. 'History is a shrine,' he writes in his gorgeous, crisp lyrics, but 'sometimes a scar is neither a street / nor a story, but a hyphen, a single line.' Duong uses his lines of poetry, playful yet tragic, smooth yet jagged, to unfold a uniquely hyphenated experience. The external existence of America, with its pills and malls, parallels his internal quest. Son of a refugee father who fled from Vietnam, the poet seeks to understand the previous generation's overshadowing experience. With charisma and craft, he explores his inherited contradictions—and we come with him, toward the unity of that gleaming pond."
　　　　　　—Molly Peacock, author of *The Widow's Crayon Box*

"*At the End of the World There Is a Pond* is a momentous debut collection and a dazzling tribute to the ambivalence of living. Steven Duong is not the first writer to attend to the apocalyptic tenor of contemporary existence, but he might be the first to do it with language this exuberant, particular, and humorous. These poems delight, surprise, and dive deeply into tricky relational waters, keeping us attuned to a sparkling aliveness even as we chart the true darkness of despair. I love this book for its playfulness and its grace, its sharpness and its tenderness; as a whole, it has added new layers to my understanding of the role of literature in survival. Winsome, finely wrought, funny, and profound, *At the End of the World There Is a Pond* is terrific company for the tumult of all times."　　　　　　—Gabrielle Bates, author of *Judas Goat*

"In poems striking, humorous, and assured, Steven Duong turns and turns the world over again until we are seen anew. How admirable and affirming this belief in language to charm us into fresh relationships with our bodies, our inner provinces. This is poetry from a teeming intellect deserving of our most serious attention. The velocity and music of this book will steady you far into your days." —Major Jackson, author of *Razzle Dazzle*

"I am grateful for Steven Duong's *At the End of the World There Is a Pond*, a brilliant book that is equal parts torment and torpor, but not without recompense and hope. I am grateful for its smart, strange patterning of coronations and abdications, how the speaker is the 'king of not killing / myself' and the 'king of not drinking bleach,' how drugs are 'dethroned . . . with a finger' and guillotines feature in dreams. These poems may not always want to be in our world, but I always want to be in theirs."
—Natalie Shapero, author of *Popular Longing*

"Steven Duong writes with a relentless precision that could be deemed ruthless if not for an equally unending tenderness. Swimming in the aquarium core of this fluid, shimmery collection are questions of how to tend, how to make art and expansive life in a world often committed to utter unmaking. Duong teaches us that humor is another form of grace, that formal dexterity is nothing without emotional depth, and that love is perhaps not enough, yet still worth striving, diving, singing for."
—Chen Chen, author of *Your Emergency Contact Has Experienced an Emergency*

"Not waving, not drowning, Steven Duong's poems are leaps—of mind and heart; of creaturely imagination; of metamorphosis and memory; of pain, whiplashing consciousness, and bighearted voyaging. These are rich, surprising poems—odes to friendship, to rappers; alert to and honoring difficulty, diasporic hauntings, our piscine ancestors, aqueous comrades, and damaged hearts. Duong isn't afraid to sink—into the mire of bad feeling, into impasse; nor is he afraid to leap—into dazzling figures, jokes, hymns, new worlds emerging from the bottom out. As he writes, 'The only way in is down.' Duong is a poet who seeks forms adequate to a life vibrating with complexity: his ghazals and sonnets and odes and capacious unspoolings are equally arresting and delighting. Pondering 'an invasive species of love,' Duong writes what one might have thought impossible, intimate poems of the Anthropocene. Mark-maker, soothsayer, both a plumber of depths and a delicate floater on tricky surfaces, Duong writes poems according to the soul's calendar. This is a poet alive to ruin and what's beyond ruin—even when it's another form of ruin ('the way a catfish hears / the river singing for all the things / it's drowned'). Worlds end every day but not all at once and not in the same way. Wallace Stevens wrote of the palm at the end of the mind; Duong gives us the pond at the end of the world."

— Maureen N. McLane, author of *More Anon*

"*At the End of the World There Is a Pond*, where time is measured in zodiac animals. Steven Duong's heart-wrenching lyric captures global wanderings, a history of substance use, the legacies of war and displacement across generations, and throughout, a novel unfurls via sonnets. At its core, the poems are testament to surviving one's familial history, family, and life. 'I am the king of not killing / myself,' the speaker says, in a collection organized by types of aquatic bodies: jumpers, swimmers, sinkers, and floaters. Duong documents love in a parent's face as 'an invasive species,' deftly revealing the complicated interplay of Eastern and Western manifestations of care and tenderness. Through these poems, I find a map for how to survive various kind of private, personal, and environmental extinction events. I find myself on the page, in a mirror with others who still alive, who have survived, just like me."

—Diana Khoi Nyugen, author of *Root Fractures*

"*At the End of the World There Is a Pond* is a spectacular book of poems. Leaping from country to country, the speaker navigates the 'blue phase' of the earth, the distance between kin, spiraling physical and mental health, and the 'avenues of hunger' that beckon and tempt all of us. Sorrow is braided, though, with a playfulness—at the level of wit, imagination, and language. These are three-dimensional poems. As is the speaker: he builds new kinships, is self-aware, and delights in fleeting beauty and peace. Steven Duong is an immensely gifted poet. I look forward to teaching this book."

—Eduardo C. Corral, author of *Guillotine*

AT THE END OF THE WORLD
THERE IS A POND

AT THE END OF THE WORLD
THERE IS A POND

POEMS

STEVEN DUONG

W. W. NORTON & COMPANY
Independent Publishers Since 1923

For information about permission to reproduce selections from this book, write to Permissions, W. W. Norton & Company, Inc., 500 Fifth Avenue, New York, NY 10110

For information about special discounts for bulk purchases, please contact W. W. Norton Special Sales at specialsales@wwnorton.com or 800-233-4830

Manufacturing by Versa Press
Production manager: Anna Oler

ISBN 978-1-324-08678-9

W. W. Norton & Company, Inc., 500 Fifth Avenue, New York, NY 10110
www.wwnorton.com

W. W. Norton & Company Ltd., 15 Carlisle Street, London W1D 3BS

1 2 3 4 5 6 7 8 9 0

for Lucie

*In studying the jumping behavior of guppies, it was clear
to Soares and Bierman that the fish did not jump to escape
predators—neither were they jumping out of the tank to acquire
food. This left the possibility that the guppies were jumping out
of the water as a means of seeking another body of water.*
—KATE BARRINGTON, "Aerial Jumping in the
Trinidadian Guppy"

Jump, jump, trampoline, fly to where you want to be!
—KERO KERO BONITO, "Trampoline"

·

CONTENTS

III. THE SINKERS

IV. THE FLOATERS

AT THE END OF THE WORLD
THERE IS A POND

AT THE END OF THE WORLD THERE IS A POND

The water is wet, the fish finned
& wriggling.

> Either that or the water wiggles,
> keeping the fish fed
> & watered.

Or no—the water feeds on
the fish, their upstream exodus, the wet

whittling the fish to bone.

When my mother came here, she whistled a song
for the fish back home.

> *Finally. Finally. Finally.*

She had been lied to about certain things.

> The nature of violence.
> That water wets itself, that fish
> whet larger fish.

The line across her back marks
where doctors took her dorsal fin.

Or no. Her heart.
It wriggles alone in its tank,

beating itself like a fish
               against a dock, a finned

atomic clock.

~

When I left my country, I packed enough pills
for a year. My year of green & orange.

          In Chiang Rai, it is Burning Season.
                    The farmers host fires
          before the next crop.

          What the fuck is a necessary violence?

At the bottom of the pond is another pond.
With the right gear, you can go there.

          I have only ever been diving
          in fresh water, where snails are moss-

swallowed fists, where men toss their breath
     like nickels in a well.

                    The only way to sink
                    is to empty yourself.

The only way in is down.

~

I am beginning to feel optimistic about the aquarium.
The plants are growing like weeds, the fish

    like fish.

        When I was five, my father kept ten
        gallons in the kitchen, kept them

well, the glass clean,
the water finned & willowy—still

there were jumpers.

        If a fish focuses, it might become either a javelin
        or a mother. The end of one world

might spell
    the beginning of another, as in

there are pills you take & pills that take you.

Or no.

The End. A clean finish,
        the fishing boats fleeing at night,

the water teeming with life.

I wanted to understand the jumpers until I did.

I

THE JUMPERS

ORIGIN STORY

In the Year of the Hare I saw in your face
an invasive species of love which said
If this is how you live your life
    perhaps you should live it elsewhere
& so I did

I lived it big

    I lived it elsewhere

I placed my belongings
in a waterproof shell
said goodbye to the Asian carp
the kudzu vines
the bark beetles stripping the coast
of music

I became an invader myself

a pathogen with survival traits

I flooded the Mekong with plum wine
burned a hole in Shaanxi Province

I opened a small business
delivering small mammals
to the owners of piranhas

& when it went under I sank
to the bottom of Lake Malawi

rose finned & wealthy

The lake became a pond
became a tank became a bowl

I lived & I lived

For you I did it elsewhere

NOVEL

In a Chinese café disguised as a French
café I am writing a novel with no white
characters. My white friend says it's beautiful.
My brown friend says it's a suicide note
with an overreliance on voice & no semblance
of plot. There is a mother, a son, a small
drug problem. Betta fish are a motif.
Like them, the mother & son are born
to break each other. They are predators,
even when there is nothing left to hunt.
The dialogue is sparse because they speak
with their eyes. Their eyes look like my eyes,
just slightly off, like an image in a pond
made foreign by the mouth breaking its surface.

COMPANION

The last person I told was
a stranger. He had one too,
a gnarled thing with bruises
for eyes. He took it with him
on business trips, let it sleep at
the foot of every hotel bed
in Guangzhou. Plum wine & two
Percocets for breakfast, no lunch,
no dinner. When its teeth
got long, his second wife trimmed
them. What about you?
he asked. Who do you have?
No one, I told him. He still thinks
he was my first. I never had to tell
the real first. She could hear it in
my voice the way a catfish hears
the river singing for all the things
it's drowned. You're not slick,
she said. I see you with your plateful
of bones, kneeling by the water
like a saint. You're not a saint.
You're starving. Listen to me,
baby boy. Stop feeding that thing.

ODE TO FUTURE HENDRIX IN THE YEAR OF THE GOAT

This blessing should include a Styrofoam cup,
an ocean of sweetness to fill said cup.

Niceties & diamond grins. May your dirty money
be wrapped in red. May your dirty hands cup

something clean, clean meaning Amiri jeans
with the Saint Laurent jacket (XL, mink hood), cup

meaning anything that gives its shape to the weight
it carries. For example: the king in my ear is a cup

full of spirits. Hungry ones. *I know the devil is real.*
Ragged throat. Slur-breath. Deathwish hiccupping

across the drums like an '83 Cutlass Supreme
(candy paint, custom Forgiatos), cupping

the moon in rearview. May we one day grow as
full as the moons behind your tongue, a couple

grams of white & some purple to chase it home.
No past. No future. Just two bottomless cups.

LAKE MALAWI POSTCARD

I'm trying to be a man with broad shoulders.
Things get heavy, Bee. Sometimes I lose my
shit in a cabin on a lake. Too many flies. Too many
bodies crash-landed in the dirt. I get antsy. I take
my drugs dutifully with my breakfast, wedding the pills
that won't take to the eggs that won't give. A man
can hope. A man can wilt his hands into fists, his fists
into prayers. Some things a fist can do, a prayer
wouldn't dream of. But is the opposite true?
The opposite of Coke is Pepsi. The opposite of saying
is doing. When all is said & done, I resay, redo,
refresh the page until it crashes. I get heavy,
Bee. I'm trying to be a man with hope in hand.

ANATOMY

My friend the songstress says there's no
point in writing nature poems anymore,
not unless you drown the verses in smoke
& oil & organophosphates—the Anthropocene
demands a new syntax. These days,
she says, the body is everything
it isn't. The corpse is still a body, but so is
the rapper's discography & the bicameral
legislature & the newly incorporated biotech
startup splicing the DNA of moon jellies
with that of house geckos & corn, because
in every line of work there is an instrument
called metaphor, that mode of torture in
which you bend a body until it says what
you want it to, this body, like all bodies, a set
of desires with an open mouth. Arrogance,
she says, is believing we're the only mouths
starved for answers. She says all this, knowing
that when I reached for cereal this morning
& shook a gecko from its perch—a tumble,
a yelp, a reptilian glint of dismay, pissed &
primordial beneath webbed lids—I began to sing
the Saigonese folk song my mother taught me,
the one about the bickering gecko brothers
who wage war across the walls until one loses
his tail. That when the grey lump of flesh
brushed my hand on its way down, I clambered
for metaphor, something to explain why brothers
rend each other limb from limb as the village

songstress watches from the kitchen, rewiring their
din of blood & teeth, of flies & crickets dying
one by one in the night, into a thing with a tune.

EXTINCTION EVENT #6 AT THE
SHANGHAI OCEAN AQUARIUM

Unfortunately, the horseshoe crab is not
that upturned bowl behind the glass
but the mess of legs beneath it, whirring
like gears in some large & expensive clock.
A surgery of legs, so sharp, so painfully precise in
how they wound the sand. That Cambrian crawl.
That lurch of blades. It's more than enough
to unseat me from my throne of good living,
this great hall in which empty things move
as if full, where suits of armor carry ghosts
& ancestral aches & other deep & primitive
losses, just never all these legs. No. What I see
is too much, too many. Which leads me to you.
This name we share. This fossil record, this love
written again & again in the dirt. Imagine a door
at the bottom of the ocean. What of us escapes
the end? What scuttles into the light, tongueless
& proud of it, tearing up the seafloor with
its thousand stupid limbs?

MONGOL CHESS SET, BRASS & JADE (1644)

A pale green field. Our ranks swollen
with livestock. Horse-pawns. Camel-knights.
All hooves & teeth—this is how we make

our love. You sheath your sword.
I leave my halberd at home. No arms here
but our own. Two kings, one crown.

Our queens, the lion-dog & elephant,
guard the soul's innermost temple.
Mine, forgetting her tusks are teeth,

goes hungry. Still, we throw bodies
at bodies. We flank. We flail. We open fire
like it's a door, like it leads somewhere

soft & spacious & not somewhere
on fire. Our bishops die young. Our rooks
are caskets with carved hinges

we leave shut. It is safer this way.
To make our wars with love. All hope
& hurry. A pale green field.

VENEERS

Like all good conquerors, the Burmese had the foresight to leave picturesque ruins. Americans find ruins fascinating because we fear being laid low, our great monuments atomized & tossed to the wind, our lawns left unruly, unkempt, untrimmed. The Buddha, crowned in crowshit, makes us think thoughts we ought to think more of, like, perhaps it is not my children who will reap the fruits of my labor, or, my house sits upon another house's bones. I am wine-drunk in the temple again. Against the grand hopes of my ancestors, all this red brick makes me think of Harvard. A well-fed stray snarls at me & I meet its challenge, my sneer sticky with Pepsi-Cola, my veneers stickiest. Fake recognize fake. Yes, that's me in the front camera's shithole gaze, razor burns & teeth yellowing like linens. In high school, I smashed my front teeth on a metal bar. The dust looked exactly like cocaine. It didn't hurt, but for a month, my half-love kissed a ruined mouth, a gate breached again & again by the tongues of barbarians. This was strange & exciting. When I finally got them fixed, she went back to what she knew best, the pipe, the pills, the man, & I kept on living, smiling my foreign smile, tossing it like a coin. How lucky to have been kissed at all. How American to be ruined then whole then ruined again.

THE BLACK SPEECH

at the bus station in Sukhothai
you see a man with a long
snaking poem wrapped around
his arm in what looks until further
research like Elvish
further research meaning Google
who says No no no my love
that's the Black Speech of Mordor
one of many made-up
           languages you have yet to learn
& did you know Tolkien once
received from a fan a goblet
engraved with this very poem
           how he used it as an ashtray
because even in his world
of worlds some tongues
are fit only for burning
& when a different war was
on he trained horses to run
toward small arms fire
knowing that with enough
practice anything can learn
to love the sound of sharp things
making soft things softer
           which makes a tattoo rig the best
pen for this long snaking poem
written between mortar strikes
in pastures of barbed wire

but please
     don't let my data mine limit you
     you too are an engine
     of remembering

remember

years before he shot himself
your kung fu teacher gave you a paperback *Hobbit*
said if you loved *Rings*
     you would at least like this one

remember

he smiled the way a king might smile
he kicked the way a gun might kick

& when he moved to the east coast
you felt like a car without doors

& when his daughter attended that school
she was five   then six

remember

you who never attended their funerals
you who are twenty-something & may never
again see a classroom
     crownless boy

allow me to spoil one ending for you

three days from now you will round the curve
of a mountain road
90 kg of metal   looping an asphalt barrel

        you will seek the definite end of a straight line

        you will come to with flies in your
mouth
& dirt in your eyes

& when you remove your helmet
a moth will fly out

you will mistake your bruises
for foreign objects lodged inside
you & feel   for ten seconds
like a good host

you will think of the days you wanted most
to leave but were too ashamed to go

you will feel very far away from the countries
you've invented
        in the sand   in the snow

remember

how some words
cannot be chewed down
how your father heard the news
    & voted for another round

three rings for the tongueless kings

the king in the sky
the king under the mountain
the king of bruised stone

there is no language alone
that can eulogize the living

II

THE SWIMMERS

TRAVEL BLOG

Mars smells like piss.

Mercury is an Israeli settlement.

There is an active shooter situation on Venus,
whose moons appear to have been deleted.

Dr. Nguyen reports that the gas giants
have merged into one supermassive ball.

Because our sun is shrinking, she says,
supermassive means less & less each year.

Elon Musk is a supermassive bitch.

Transmission from Mons Olympus:
the astronomers are tired of the classics.

The new planet's name will be 鬼才.

鬼才 was a Tang Dynasty poet who died
broke, strung-out on ether.

Pluto smells like piss.

I am glad to be leaving this place.

GOOD DOG

is what I say to my Siamese
    fighting fish when I pet her,

because a dog is anything small
& good to me. She nibbles my finger,

breaks no skin but
the water's. This morning,

I took two pills & felt
little. Now, I feel lots. I love this thing

of mine. Her fins are good.
    Her tail is too. Good dog.

ORDNANCE

At the museum I learn I am as tall as
some bombs (5"7'). The bombs in
question are dumb bombs, which means
they do not question gravity. They just
land where they land, bury what they
can. Placed in rows they look something
like soldiers. Dumb soldiers. The placard explains
how all bombs used to be dumb, how the term
was coined retroactively by whoever made them
smart, taught them about lasers, thermo-
dynamics, critical theory, all the things
a contemporary bomb must know to
stay competitive in a growing field.
War was simpler when my dad lived here.
It was called Saigon then & the bombs were so dumb
they didn't even know it. All they had to do
was their jobs. Christ. This place has no damn
AC. The casualties are colorized, the tourists
are foreigner than me, & Lennon serenades us
on a loop, asking us every three & a half minutes
to imagine no possessions. My phone dings.
Take museum with salt, texts Ba. It's propaganda.
Fish sauce, I reply. I send him photos:
me standing in front of a nearly
forgotten apartment, an elementary school,
a wildlife sanctuary. I allow him to imagine me
happy. I tell him on Tuesday I fed mangoes
to a ten-year-old elephant. I do not tell him
it was recovering from a land mine blast.

I do not tell him his friend groped me last night
at the bar, & I definitely do not tell him I am
a communist. The world is a list of things
I keep from my father. Before I leave, I run
my hands over the shell of another
sleeping bomb. But I'm not the only one,
sings John. We're dumb as hell. Full of hurt.

NOVEL

I added white characters. Not for the white
reader but for myself. I just needed
the mother & son to feel watched, to feel watched
myself as I wrote my way around their lives.
Two fish in a tank. A tank being a glass box with
a filter. Filtration is crucial. It is possible
for fish to drown, though not betta fish, whose
labyrinth organs allow them to borrow freely
from the sky. You can keep them in bowls,
rice paddies, pickle jars. You can watch
them tear each other fin from fin without
worrying about the water choking them.
Which is what I wanted. To watch them break
each other & know they did it alone.

OXYCODONE

I find you in the dark between hours.
I don't always know what to do with you.

> When I don't know what to do with you,
> I pocket you, swathe you in cotton.

You, pocketed in swaths of cotton.
You, sea-green breath on my shoulder this morning.

> Breathing sea-green against the shoulder of morning,
> the clam is, of course, as happy as a clam.

Today the clams are happy to be clams.
Tomorrow is a pond at the edge of the sea.

> Tomorrow, my feet in the pond, yours in the sea,
> we become little doors, always opening.

I will always open my door to you
in the hours between darkness.

UNTOGETHER

& sleep-thin, we ride into the crawlspace
of January, meet I-80's long blank stare with
our eyes red & our needs seated between
us like strangers: countless, quiet,

unmet. We know history
is written by the warmly dressed,
that the poets will freeze in their
        Camrys, & so we hustle.

It is dark now.

We've agreed to stop belonging to
each other in the dark. We must be &
long for new things, things pleasing to the ear,
things bought & sold at market price.

For a long time, our mothers were
toothpicks dangling from the mouths
of Watertown &
Chinatown. Sharp things
        chewed down. Which is what

we're becoming. Eventually, we'll all be
our mothers remixed, played raw against the city's din.
Flash your luck, says
the dark to our brainstems. Let your teeth

be celebrations, little Tếts, loud, lawless,
obnoxiously gold. You'll miss your paychecks.
Your flights, your families. So what?

You're still
in motion, aren't you?

Go!

At dawn, the light is yours. Even
if you want nothing to do with it.

CURFEW

I am spending the day in bed
reading recipes for
molotov cocktails

tonight I'll burn paper
in the name of love
raise two armies on Venmo

I hope to see a Tesla kiss a brick wall

it's a fucking chore to live in this nation
of content creators
filling the void
        with The Void

but I do it

& when Florida slips into the waves
I pray for the nail salons

& when the expat compares his home
to a phantom limb
I ignore him

I write a poem for the white hoods
& a poem for my dad
        it's the same poem

I kiss a brick wall

I light incense for no one in particular
allow the smoke to unionize

the world is a sure thing
& we are only possibilities

what is a citizen but
     a) an evening with filed teeth
     b) an hour full of smaller hours
     c) a red line gunning for the bottom

fuck all that

dear council of smoke I love you
but no longer require
   your show of hands

I bear the scepter
I wear the crown

I am the king of not killing
myself & will not be dethroned

that's a promise
a five-year plan

as in
     1) in years one & two I will continue as I am
     2) in year three I will make a change
     3) years four & five will surely be glorious

when Dean told me I had to stay alive
as long as he was alive
        I said okay   I said it twice

like any good soothsayer
I said what I had to believe

I said
in five years I will be a good ruler
a nail technician   a licensed soothdoer

I will stop shutting the door on the angel

I will deserve the wings
the lights
        the steady check

when the markets fall & the workers
pop their bubbly

I will die old
        poet laureate
        of wherever they find me

o council
old habits dye hearts

once I cut up the knight of swords
& rolled him into a cigarette filter

once my parents taught me their
parents' word for death
        but I'm blanking on it

how is death a promise if you can't
even break it

it's the living

        Gaby is living

Dean is living

this year I will handle
        the living with care

THE SINGER

She wants a love that falls as fast as a body
from the balcony, & so do we, only
we can't say it out loud like she does, rattling
in our ears like loose change, like rust-bitten
wind chimes in a storm, never seeking the notes
but finding them anyway. What is love
but a stained driveway, the body but its after-
math? Ones & zeroes cut raw in the glass,
deriving nothing from nothing. Whose fingers
crammed down whose throat? How many impacts
until FIST becomes FIFTH? There's a calculus to
hurt, sings the singer, & we believe her, hurtling
down I-80 like the last words of a dying
star, the night washing us down with bourbon.

THE POET

Our nights, washed down with bourbon, are nothing more
than reenactments. Each migration from bed
to car, front seat to back—a reprint of some
flight path devised by our moon-eyed forebears.
A man detects mortar fire in Korea.
You mourn him on a Saturday, a week
since the doctor detected the friendly fire
in his cells. A woman is caught before she can
escape Saigon by boat. Next week, the pills
catch me before I can escape her story
by rope. We carry small wars on our backs,
writes the poet. We can't explain this. We can't
explain us. You trace the white trails on my arm
as you pull into park, so sure their ends are dead.

THE FAILED REFUGEE

Try again, she says. There are no dead ends
in a flight path. Every in is an out. Every
one is a two laid low. In Little Saigon,
she buys you a jade heart, me a waving cat.
As if trinketed in luck, we might hustle
the CIA spooks into haunting us, into
breaking our falls & dulling our knives, letting
our filial negligence slide. We abandon
the car & bask in the drunk stutter of street-
lamps, deaf to the stars—those uncles tut-tutting
in their shrines. Sometimes history is a shrine
we plant together. It sleeps beneath the soil
like a land mine. Sometimes a scar is neither a street
nor a story, but a hyphen, a single line.

THE UNNAMED GHOST

Her story—a bone-white line across her throat.
Given enough time, she says, are all stories
not ghost stories? She is like us, only
lighter (for being dead), & so she clings
to the air like incense smoke. The moment we
swill down our pills she is gone. Her question hangs
in the dark, quiet & alive. You squeeze my hand.
The thing with incense is it eats itself
alive to send a message. Here we are!
We syllables of smoke! We animals,
shaved & sedated! Give us wings & we'll
fly on up. Give us tongues & we'll misspeak
ourselves. You may as well give us the crown
because we've already swallowed the jewels.

III

THE SINKERS

HO CHI MINH CITY

So much of this country's goodness faces
the water. The doorless café. The white faces

of clocks. I keep a sixth-floor room,
notching up lagers with the expats, facing

weak spliffs on the roof. It's a life. I try to hit
two pages by noon, & when I fail, I wash my face

& head to the market, throwing paper where the
noise curdles like milk, where the pinched faces

of the vendors, those uncles hawking fake
Audemars Piguets, look nothing like my face.

To see the seedling as the son of the tree
is unscientific. Once, my mom faced

a small fine for smuggling bougainvillea cuttings.
She wanted her first country's flowers to face

her new country's sun & was ready to pay
for it. These are the only times I see her face

in mine, these strange & stubborn currents
she rides. You have the language & the face,

the hostel owner tells me—why not make a life here?
The dollar is good. The women wear the faces

they are born with. He uncaps his beer by mouth.
I dive to the bottom of my thirst before surfacing.

What else can I tell you? I am me, a man
named after men. I wear their bravest faces.

NOVEL

I am nearing the heart of it. Some bridges
between parents & children resist meaning
until crossed. When I was nine I crushed
a guppy underfoot & mourned for weeks
is a lie I like to tell. It was my mother
who cried, she who taught me to lie, & so
the mother & son in the novel are liars too.
They lie in poorly lit rooms & kitchenettes,
to their lovers, their landlords, themselves.
I am not yet sure what kind of lie the novel
is, but I tell it. It wasn't the son who killed
his fish. All he did was keep it behind
the glass, & when it saw what it wanted,
it jumped. It was free before it was dead.

SOUTH XIZANG ROAD POSTCARD

Look Bee

here's October with its oil-slick sky
its AC on the fritz

this view from that window
    the Starbucks & the dragon-gate

spring-green lovers gliding downstreet
in matching Balenciagas

O Balenciagas!

Triple-S's with the clear soles
frames Chanel
jeans Off-White
Chrome Hearts laser-cut & holy
on their tennis chains

O Shanghai!

these avenues in grayscale
umbrella-skins
    & lanterns bobbing like fish
a bellyup brand of beauty
    malls toppled fifty times
    in fifty years

their stories told
to disappear   a curved scrim of light
announcing Big Truths

like
to write is to write & unwrite
& write again in code

O Bee!

I just know you'd fucking hate it here

every night I pray the city pressure-cooks
my thoughts into dreams

    but they never seem to come

perhaps it's because the neighbors are in love
perhaps it's because they splice samples of their love
    through the drywall
& seem to have no careers of any kind

no barriers to loving one another
    in eight by twelve square feet of comfort
    so close to dawn
to the glorious hollow
between my ears & my brain

that lonely lightbulb on its lonely string
    flickering itself to dust

O dust!

what I'm saying is I want you

MAO

is loyalty so much to ask for
a small but dedicated following
on Twitch

I am a tired young man
king of not drinking bleach
first chairman of cool heads

this isn't a pill cutter my friend
it's a guillotine for insects
who've betrayed me

if any of you are listening
please mail me drugs
I'd like nothing more
than to be full of Vicodin
& red wine
tracing the bones of
Zhoujiazui Road streaming
Uzi leaks through a VPN

I cannot tell a lie
but someone has to

the sign by Exit 4 reads
MAO ZEDONG'S FORMER RESIDENCE

nowadays he lives in my wallet
no one carries him here but me

when I try to pay for oolong tea
the chairman is so crisp he bleeds
my little finger

EVEN IN TIMES OF GLOBAL PANIC I AM A NARCISSIST

as my fever rides on
to a brighter & snowier peak
the tyrant of my heart texts me a BBC
article about the novel coronavirus

its humble origins at a wet market
its humble hijacking of
bats snakes dromedaries
    & the hospitalizations spiking
now among aunts &
uncles who look if you squint
like my aunts & uncles

in this case novel means
as of yet unwritten
corona means garland wreath crown

small fealties sworn in cell beds & protein
cathedrals to kings of imaginary kingdoms

these lands where I am always breaking
what I do not get into
more easily ingestible truths
pills to powders
powders to finer powders

I collect thank yous in every language
& file my teeth on them
arranging the dust in lines as
     orderly as legislation

so when the virus arrives at last in the city
of me I will be a fountain of accessibility
a most gracious host

my love is worried which worries me

& of course I imagine dying
the easiest breakdown to imagine
the body finally giving up
its thank yous
becoming the sum of its syllables
bone shards bleached by salt by sun
by everyone

I arrange a hospital visit
I do not have the novel coronavirus

the doctor dopes me up thirty
minutes after I dope myself up
& so I ride home in a
chariot of blue light
synaptic clefts closing like liquor stores

an avenue of hungers blurs
    into an avenue of thirsts
pink-light districts & watering holes
where tourists light
small pyres & catch their flights

as I round the corner
the corner rounds me

I send lovely but uncomforting texts

I withhold sensitive information

in the cracked touchscreen of night
I convert Celsius to Fahrenheit

FOR THE LUCKY GOLD CAT AT THE REGISTER
OF PHO 888

Dear friend. Narcissist that I am, I see
you for what we are: two lonely little lords.
	By this I mean we govern small things alone.
Our angers are brief, our griefs are angry, & here
we sit, batting our paws again & again
	at what we can't quite hold, staring it down,
making it holy. Holy the mint leaves. Holy
the busboy. Holy the hole in the wall & the
	woman behind it cooking lunch & dinner
specials for Des Moines's finest, each of them holy
too, because in our country there is no difference
	between waving & beckoning. Every greeting
is a business venture. All luck is good luck.
A coin in the hand is worth ten in the fountain,

& you know how these waters coin us. Gold fronts
on plastic teeth. The oldest money youth
	can buy. To mint yourself new is to make yourself
tender, to hatch fresh names for what ails you,
the way the koi behind the shop does for the pennies
	ruining its pondwater. Chokestars. The bad shine.
My ungentle sunken lovers. You who bleed
my blood. I could wax on, but as you know, red-
	collared comrade, face beat for the gods, there's bank
to be made, white envelopes to gut like fish.
See you when the rent is paid. Until then, please
	name me in your prayers. Dear friend. Coin me

lucky. Hustle me into the hands of those
who would drown me in grants and stipends.

OUR LOVE

is thick & slow & heavy, like cement
poured down a rabbit's warren.

Choke-love. Broke-love.
It sprouts in a valley

of crumpled receipts.
It peoples a fishing boat

    & bleeds the Pacific.

Every word chambered
in our love's mouth

stumbles out as drunk
& mispronounced

as our love. Bright thing. Brittle thing.
There it sits, unblessed,

uneaten, farming dust
    on the family altar.

We even find it between
the drowning fish &

its pond. There is no softer collapse
than our love, no

suffocation as foreign
or familiar. Between us, who is the

waterlogged body that breaks
the pondskin, scales full of moon?

Who is the moon?

ODE TO PLAYBOI CARTI IN THE YEAR OF THE DOG

When I kick up the treble, something in your voice cracks
like a sun ten seconds from going red dwarf, from cracking

the sky open like a pint of your favorite. When I punch down
the mid, the star offs itself, spilling all your firecracker

adlibs into the street, the beat a kind of festival, each WHAT!
& WHOA! a cork popping off to welcome the crack

of dawn—one last toast to the season's famished ghosts, to
the year well bruised on your wrist with its cracked

watch face, its coat of stars. Before I can up the bass, Ba says,
Sounds bad, change it. He wrinkles his nose, refuses to crack

his best Californian smile, so I flash my own, toothy &
    off-white.
I let your 808s thump on like mortars, your snares crack

like small arms. He snorts, grimaces, boots up the radio.
See the lines in his face, those runes wrinkling to the crackle

of distant stations. They know that silence is white, that noise
is red, & it takes a whole lot of red to sunset a galaxy, to crack

the safe of good fortune. Before me, he was like you. He knew
all the lyrics to joy. He never let quiet slip through the cracks.

NOVEL

The son is writing one too. He writes the
way I sometimes do, swinging the lyric
cudgel with abandon, waxing elegiac
for his mother & her brothers & the war
they didn't die in. *In my mother tongue,*
he writes, *the words for country and water are
the same.* For a little too long, I thought these
thoughts profound. I believed myself the sole
practitioner of a magic called Having Parents
For Whom I Could Speak, & from this belief
sprang my whole life, ready-made like Athena
with its arms & armor. *War, then, is two rivers
bleeding into the sea*—these lines, they belonged
once to me. The son I couldn't help but be.

SONNET LASER-ENGRAVED ON THE 30-ROUND MAGAZINE OF A BUSHMASTER XM15-E2S RIFLE PURCHASED AT BROWNELLS, INC. IN GRINNELL, IOWA, FEBRUARY 2012

All the time I am losing teeth. A grinful
of pale horses looses itself each night
from the stable in my jaws, seeking heat &
taking it. I am ashamed I cannot recall
their names. Too many releases. But the bodies
they bear, how they hollow my mouth & nestle
inside, how they jacket my throat in shine—

how can I forget? I cannot forget

that loss is a thing with hooves. That it grazes
skin & spine. There are only two sides
to a stampede, those who run & those who bleed,
& all I can do is hold them. Carry their coats.
Conceal them from each other until they bolt,
like the beasts they are, for warmer holes to lie in.

SONNET SANDBLASTED INTO A SEVEN-YEAR-OLD HEADSTONE IN NEWTOWN VILLAGE CEMETERY, CONNECTICUT, MARCH 2019

Small stones directed under high pressure
to curve the face of something larger. Your name
beside your daughter's. You chose granite when
she was shot, & so I am granite: a hard summit
of devotion, losing ground each year to acid
rain & soil erosion. Though I am stone,

I am not unfeeling. I cannot unfeel

your name. Hers either. I would have preferred
just one. Two is the heaviest thing I know,
& I know so much. Four minutes, ten magazines.
Six years, seven more. I wish you stayed home,
Jeremy. I wish I was an igneous rock
of no significance. But I am yours.
We are magnificent. They crown us in lilies.

BREAK IN CASE OF EXTINCTION EVENT

when the earth enters its blue phase
& the rivers leave their beds
unmade

when hurricanes pull undersea
your father's father's
fishery

& the sea shakes down the sky
& the insulin flows like oil

when you stop dreaming of catfish
with pearls for eyes
   & pill-cutter mouths

when the South unfurls
its newborn coast like
a series of ferns

& your mother toasts her cardiac surgeon
& the savanna continues to burn

when we kayak down the road
to loot the pharmacy
named for the oligarch

when we unplug the doomsday clock
& guillotine the clocksmiths
in Central Park

& your little brother wins the war
& nothing more

this is when

then & only then
& only then

IV

THE FLOATERS

LABYRINTH

I am beginning to think Icarus was a bad refugee
the star that did him in
just one vessel in a fleet of outs

there is nothing seaworthy
about the wrong dose

I am done writing about cars I never drove

out of the labyrinth / into the light

go ahead & try me
if I dethroned the percs with a finger
    what can I do with ten

the flight path has a two-book deal
but I have friends

there are ways to get what you want
without burning the house down
says the auntie to
    the auntie to the auntie

this gaptooth April with its busted spleen
my father weeds the garden while
    my uncle breathes through a tube

I am beginning to dream about guillotines

my ramshorn snails live & die in twenty gallons
whole dynasties passing
     beneath algae-kissed glass

Vietnam requires foreigners to wear masks
so I wear a mask

as soon as this check clears
I am done writing about us

BEST-CASE SCENARIO

This century ends underwater, the earth inherited by catfish
the size of sedans. The highways bloom into rivers &
    the roaches

sprout gills. Business booms. Water striders stride. The
    value of fins
skyrockets while the value of legs eats shit. The bones of
    the poets,

still belted to their Camrys, are settled by runaway
    guppies sprung
from home aquariums, which become museums the
    way Alcatraz

& Angel Island are museums, the way Japanese
    internment camps
have gift shops, My Lai four stars on Tripadvisor. By the end,
    the borders

drown themselves. Tilapia born & raised in Lake Malawi
    drive west
to kick it with Tahoe trout & Yangtze river dolphins. Fin to fin,

they make circles in a CVS parking lot, gliding like
    sunken angels
through clouds of Lexapro & Opana. Theirs is a legless future,

but like the roaches, some of us are still kicking. Everyone
who ever wanted to live is dead. The rest of us tread water.

NOVEL

I'm still looking for a title. Something sharp.
Plaintive. Load-bearing. The first one, which
I won't write here, couldn't carry me where
I had to be. It left the mother & son unmoored,
just as my own name unmoors me from what
came before: fruit markets, lycées, Nixon,
etcetera. War is a thing I read about. Saigon.
Kabul. When Jamel says write, I write. When Tak
FaceTimes me, we talk about *Survivor*, the stories
we tell to keep ourselves stranded on beaches
with who we've hurt for money. I know this
is stupid, he says, but I didn't think they'd
lie to me. I could lie to him too, but I don't.
I say his name. I tell him something lovely.

WORLDSHIP

some genius decided to gift the
community a class-A worldship

which is why we are abroad again
rootless & starving
again

at one point we were redder than blood
        says the captain's uncle
before they pronounce him dead
a possible ingredient

we are approaching what historians
call a Donner Party situation

this cold porcelain rock
with no arable soil
this newborn nation of so many mouths
        & so few farmers

our hotpot robots look a bit like Chun-Li
the born-again Koreans are planting sins

Hoa Mai the photographer
shoots Hoa Mai the performance artist

& my cousin Angie dresses her
        the old Cantonese way
oyster sauce with honey & lotus

the word LANGUAGING appears above New Saigon
in Tumblr blue & 4chan green

as rogue memoirists seize the gunnery

& the poets are singing again
of dumplings
    tongues & bubble tea
how strict their mothers
used to be

ODE TO RICO NASTY IN THE YEAR OF THE RAT

I keep a list of songs that make me cry
despite the meds. I keep a list of songs to cry

to. You're on the first but not the second.
When you rap about your hair, I cry

for your hair, the way you sharpen it into something
sharper than hair, dye it so damn blue it cries

itself new. A little bird once told me blue
songs are like tattoos. Some birds cry

when hungry or bored. Dylan named his
Cassius, which is enough to make me cry.

I imagine a great black wing, a man with the luck
knocked out of him. The last time I cried,

I really had to force it out. Ma & I were yelling
in two different languages & the crying

made use of neither. After that, I put your
old shit on. I let the 808s simmer, crying

on mute. Chemically speaking, I am drier
than I've been. Still, the poems are not a cry

for help. I don't like to use the word nasty,
but it's nasty to assume I'm always crying.

LIVINGSTONIA POSTCARD

I am trying to write plainly. I am trying not to be sad
about suede & brass. Four pockets. A decade of Torontos
on my father's back. I'm not sad, just cold & pissed, because
what I lost rides north in a white van, & when its finder stops
in Dwangwa for gas & Pall Malls, he will be infinitely
warmer than me. My loss will sleeve him. As for me, I
    am outside
the bar. The sky above me is so thick with wings the stars
seem to wink, like turn signals. This is a world in which
    a fruit bat
can, for a split second, swallow a sun. This is a world
in which sons veil themselves from their fathers. I was eighteen
once. I stuck my arm full of ink. Sleeved in suede & brass,
I kept my father at bay. Picture my ink-boy in his ink-boat.
He wears a wolfskin. His left arm dangles over the ink-sea
where his fingers brush the water—a raised blur,
a smudge in the skin. I am trying to write plainly. The
    worst nights
are my birthright. The smudge is a scar. As Ba's jacket sleeps
in Karonga, I think of the nights I spent awake, making
an ashtray of my body. I was not sad. Just cold.

UNDIASPORA

It cannot all be birds & tongues,
Steven.

Sometimes the story is a fish
making circles in its tank
on Xuân Tín Road
& the boy watching it, unaware
small broken things will be
the currency of
        the rest of his life.

He will take a blue tablet in the morning,
a white one at night, a series of blues & whites
        between morning & night.

He will tell stories.

Sometimes the story is a boot
in the back. A brick in the window.
A boat full of grieving mothers.

They are not his stories to tell,
but the boy will tell them anyway.

Because there's no conclusion,
right? No markets crashing like cymbals,
no jail time for
        expats & sex pests.

It cannot all be moons & dragons,
Steven.

Sometimes the story ends
in the lake.

TATTOO

I tattoo Maggie on game day. We attend
a school with remarkable defense in a state
where hogs outnumber us. SPILL YOUR GUTS means
tell all, leave no depth unplumbed. Once a bad lake
ruined her eye so she got a Fetty Wap
tattoo & a new eye. Once her dad raced cars.
More than once actually. His job for years
was to win. This week his daughter shelved books,
taught children to teach themselves about stars
& weird bugs, Formula One, the nature of grief.
I don't really feel it, she says. No pain. The wound
grows quietly. How about now? I say.
We do this for hours: I ask her to be honest
and she tells me she is. I'm hurting no one.

TATTOO

Tak says it hurts a lot more than last time,
so I down the voltage. There. We're golden. Left
unchecked, I'd ruin my friend, this man I love
but rarely call. At eighteen we lived lives
that barely made sense, even to us the livers.
He flew here from Delhi but his fake said
Cleveland. Don't get deported, I told him.
Cheers, he replied. We drank to as many things
as we could then: friendship, empires on fire,
the hard facts of joy. In my other language,
cute means *easy to love*. That's Tak. I can't
not love him. The man bought me a rig just so
I could carve ACAB in his leg. Anyone
who would uneasy our love is a bastard.

TATTOO

I'm still easing into this bastard love.
I draw Clay a cloud & a map & when
they say, How about a cloud map, I whip
one right up. A cloud field & a big cloud
sea. A road from Cloud A to Cloud B. Meaning
nothing, really. All I know is Clay loves
these small things & is willing to live forever
with how I imagine them. Every few days
they draw a map for their friend Trevor & Trev
sends back a poem. Or vice versa. I barely
know them but it makes me so damn happy. All
that back & forth. I carve clouds in red & black.
I imagine them floating to Nashville, Portland,
Baltimore, fat with the sort of rain we live for.

TATTOO

More salt. More fat. More rain. I live for pork
stew & five or six friends with worms for brains,
tossing the same twenty bucks back & forth
like an unpinned grenade. Happy bird day, we
sing. Lucie tells me she misses me more than birds
can possibly say. She's at a loss for birds.
Even if Dylan loaned her his parrot, she'd
be stuck there in her loss, flightless & blue
as hell. I was eighteen when I wrote her
a song called "Swell." Power chords, lofted bed,
I miss you so much I feel fucked in the head
& so on. There's a solo. My brother drums.
When I touch up my bum leg, I hum the thing
I made her. I replace the ink with more ink.

THE LIVING

We're all committed to some variation on it—it's work. We're
workers. You, me, the olive tree doomed in its bed of clay, its
near-constant shade. The dog. The newer, better dog. Even the
earwigs in the pantry. Even the earwigs outside, casing the joint,
& your uncle's stunted goldfish, & the parakeets nesting in the
substation, bumming warmth from the state, & the state too,
its substitute teachers & secret police. They're doing what your
brother's doing, what Noor & Nolan & June are doing. There's
no trick to it. It's habit. That song you can't not sing. When I say
sit tight, I'll be there in ten, what I'm saying is the ugliest cat in
America lives with its perfect kittens. Your father's water lilies,
so precious at the right hour, live with stupid, unkillable carp, &
when you drive past that tidal wave of kudzu shadowing the off-
ramp, living with everything it's choked—cypress, hickory, live
oak—can't you imagine the whole city swaddled in green? When
we're gone, we'll be gone. I promise you that. For now we pay our
bills. It's work, love. If not for yourself, do it for me. For our dogs
& our birds & our trees.

NOVEL

Not even in my dreams is it done, its plots
set, its characters lost in thoughts I once
thought. There's still that long ugly stretch I forgot
to set down (i.e., chose not to recall), the parts
that constitute the Real Thing & insist
on remaining parted, even after the limp
third act & the long-expected relapse, the mother
losing her mind, the son minding her loss,
& all those lovely sentence fragments chained
like daisies to their throats. No. Most nights,
I dream of doors in a long hallway. I know
that one belongs to me, that when I step
through it, I will arrive, finally, at my life.
Just not tonight. Perhaps another night.

ASHES AT KANDE BEACH, MALAWI

Everything is an elegy these days, chipped rings,
clipped wings. You are alive, so the pills work,

but there is something morbid in even the sunrise
on the lake, the way its reds & pinks bleed

the night behind them, putting the stars to death
& in their place a blank sky, a wordless

morning. When three geckos pull their bellies
across the wall of your cabin, you spin a prayer

for the mosquitoes, the prey with their giveaway scents
& tender limbs. You wake to a hum, thinking,

Oh shit! This must be the Great Hum, the churning
of all the submersed parts & pistons that I am,

commanding me to wake up & eat & listen to Young
Thug & Elliott Smith & love my neighbor as myself,

etcetera. That Will to Live they're always talking about.
But no. The Hum simmers to a hum, & soon enough

it's gone, & there you lie, still alive, still not dead,
still as the lake at dawn. You crack the door.

Why not? You allow the dawn to slide in, feeding
you a trick of the light, light being God's first trick,

as in, Let there be light, He said, & so we were
blinded. Look. Look at the beach shrouded

in ash. Who blackened it? Who smoked it down
to the roach & gave birth to a new

& identical beach, a phoenix hatchling swaddled
in soot? As soon as you picture wings,

a pair of them, the ash begins to shiver,
& at last you see it. Not God's first trick

but his fifth. Let the seas & skies be filled
with hungry mouths. Let the ash, bristling with shine,

be not ash at all but a million lakeflies, crash-
landed, unhumming. Let the winged be betrayed by

the wind, marooned by the sand. Let the sand throw
on its corpse coat, its most sickening ensemble,

& yes, let every embrace of sole & earth be an
elegy. Why not be dramatic? Let the birds get fat.

Let the pills get heavy. Let us not walk anywhere
without treading on grief upon grief upon grief.

I VOW TO STOP PUTTING IT MILDLY

My father voted for your father
to die.

He did this with great enthusiasm,
    animated by what he believed was
    the spirit of his own father,

a civil engineer who spent a year
in a reeducation camp.

My father put your father
    in a camp. He did this with his hands,
swiftly & without regrets, a harmonica

strapped to his neck
like a Jesus piece.

My father is the Biggie Smalls
of calculated losses,
the Bob Dylan of towns on fire.

Once, I saw in his face
an invasive species of love which said

If you really love me
    you must be someone I can love.

Twice, he translated my poems
    so his mother might
      better know me.

There is kindness here, but there
are kindnesses everywhere.

One day, I will teach my children to climb
the ladder I am always climbing.

Or I won't. There's a chance
I won't.

ACKNOWLEDGMENTS

One million dollars and a deep tissue massage to the editors and staff of the publications in which many of these poems first appeared, occasionally in other forms:

The Academy of American Poets: "The Poet," "The Singer," "The Failed Refugee," "The Unnamed Ghost"

The Adroit Journal: "Extinction Event #6 at the Shanghai Ocean Aquarium," "Livingstonia Postcard," "Ode to Future Hendrix in the Year of the Goat," "Sonnet Laser-Engraved on the 30-round Magazine of a Bushmaster XM15-E2S Rifle Purchased at Brownells, Inc. in Grinnell, Iowa, February2012"

AGNI: "Break in Case of Extinction Event," "Ode to Playboi Carti in the Year of the Dog"

The American Poetry Review: "Veneers"

Catapult: "Ashes at Kande Beach, Malawi," "Origin Story"

diaCRITICS: "Even in Times of Global Panic I am a Narcissist"

Guernica: "Ordnance"

The Indiana Review: "Best Case Scenario"

The Margins: "The Unnamed Ghost"

The Massachusetts Review: "Anatomy"

The New England Review: "Ho Chi Minh City," "I Vow to Stop Putting it Mildly"

Passages North: "Untogether"

Peach Magazine: "Travel Blog," "Worldship"

Pleiades: "Our Love"

Prairie Schooner: "Mongol Chess Set, Brass & Jade (1644)"

Protean Magazine: "Curfew"

Tupelo Quarterly: "For the Lucky Gold Cat at the Register of Pho 888"

Thanks as well to the Academy of American Poets, the University of Iowa, the Watson Foundation, and Emory University for giving me the time and support to pull all of this together.

Tony Perman, Hai-Dang Phan and Ralph Savarese, the first teachers to see me before I could see myself: I owe you worlds. Jamel Brinkley, Lan Samantha Chang, Abby Geni, and Margot Livesey: I owe you worlds as well, but for now, please accept some sonnets about an anxious young novelist. Tracie Morris, the tattoo poems are for you. And Dean Bakopoulos, I have no idea where I'd be without the sheer force of your belief. Thank you for everything.

Endless love to the friends I've made family, all of whom either appear in these pages or pored over them at my request: Nolan Boggess, Cecilia Bergman, Mira Braneck, TJ Calhoun, Jack Carbone, Maggie Dambro, June Hernandez, Sarah Khatry, Takshil Sachdev, Noor Qasim, Nitya Rayapati, and Dylan Welch. Love also to Sam Burt and Andrea Baumgartel, my first true comrades in poetry.

To Diana Khoi Nguyen, who lent this book a keen eye during its infancy: thank you for the incisive questions and surprising answers. To Ale Allen, who worked tirelessly to sharpen these poems into themselves but sharper: you're getting free tattoos for life. To Brian, who writes code, and Owen, who writes music: yours are 50% off. It's a privilege to call myself your brother.

Nothing but admiration for Jin Auh, my agent and fearless champion. Nothing but gratitude for Jill Bialosky, my brilliant editor. Without the two of you, the intrepid Laura Mucha, and the dedicated workers at W. W. Norton, these poems would still be a series of haphazardly formatted Word documents on my hard drive. Thank you for believing in them.

To my first parents, Bao and Phong, and my second parents, Jean and Mal: I will always love you.

And to Lucie, the secret heart of all my poems and stories and songs: you already know everything I could possibly tell you here. All that I am, I am for you.

ABOUT THE AUTHOR

Steven Duong is the 2023–2025 Creative Writing Fellow in Poetry at Emory University. His poems have appeared in *The American Poetry Review*, *Guernica*, and *The New England Review*, among other publications, and his essays and short fiction feature in *Astra Magazine*, *The Drift*, and *The Best American Short Stories 2024*. A graduate of Grinnell College and the Iowa Writers' Workshop, he lives in Atlanta, Georgia.